What's in this book

This book belongs to

_____

我们和大自然
Nature and us

学习内容 Contents

沟通 Communication

说说自然景物
Talk about mother nature

生词 New words

★	天	sky
★	地	land
★	云	cloud
★	山	mountain
★	海	sea
★	花	flower
★	草	grass
★	小	small
★	真	really

树	tree
石头	rock
冷	cold
热	hot
大自然	nature

句式 Sentence patterns

天真高，海真大。

The sky and the sea are really big.

跨学科学习 Project

在地图上标示地点，并认识方位

Mark places on the map and learn about their positions

文化 Cultures

中国风景景观

Scenic landscapes in China

Get ready

1 Do you like to be close to nature?

2 What do you see in the countryside?

3 Do you prefer hiking or going to the beach?

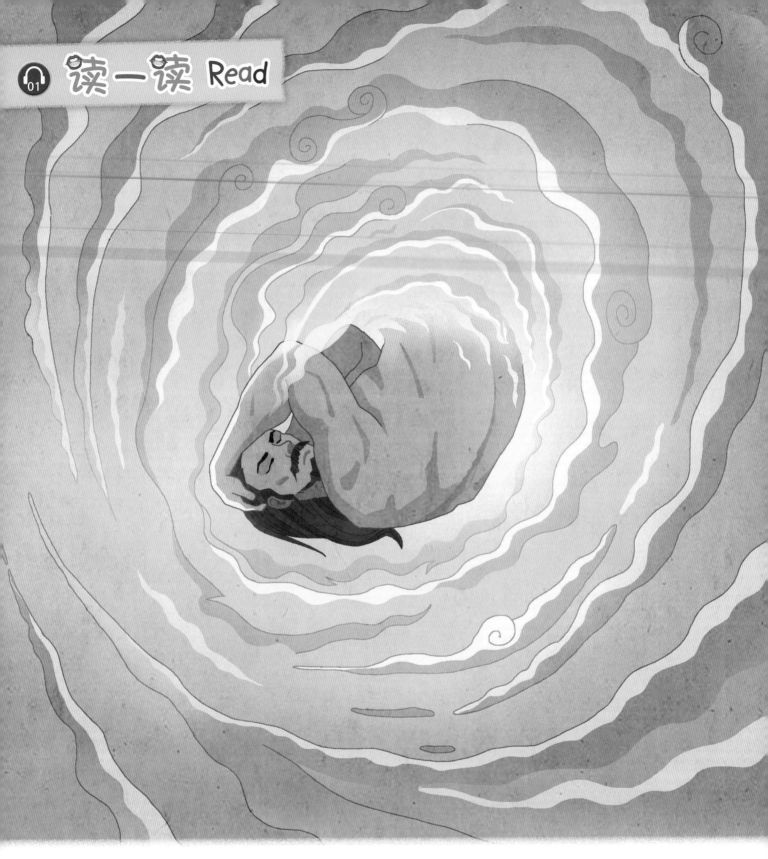

大自然是一个很大很大的圆。

tiān

天

dì

地

一天，圆分开了，上面
是天，下面是地。

云 yún

山 shān

石头 shí tou

天上有云，地上有山和石头。

山下面是海。海水很
冷，地面很热。

地上高的是树，矮的是
花，小的是草。

dà zì rán
大自然

xiǎo
小

地上还有小小的人。
大自然真奇妙！

Let's think

1 Circle six natural objects mentioned in the story.

2 Look at the pictures. Tick the ones that you like. Tell your friend the reasons.

New words

1 Learn the new words.

天

大自然

云

山

树

真热。

海

真冷。

石头

地

草

花

小

2 Match the words to the pictures. Write the letters.

a 云　　b 海　　c 花　　d 山　　e 石头　　f 草

听听说说 Listen and say

1 Listen and circle the correct answers.

2 Look at the pictures. Listen to the sto

1 它是什么？
   a   海
   b   地
   c   山

2 它是什么？
   a   天
   b   云
   c   花

3 它是什么？
   a   草
   b   花
   c   树

nd say.

你看见什么？

我看见……

Task

Recall a field trip you went on and complete the journal. Talk about it with your friend.

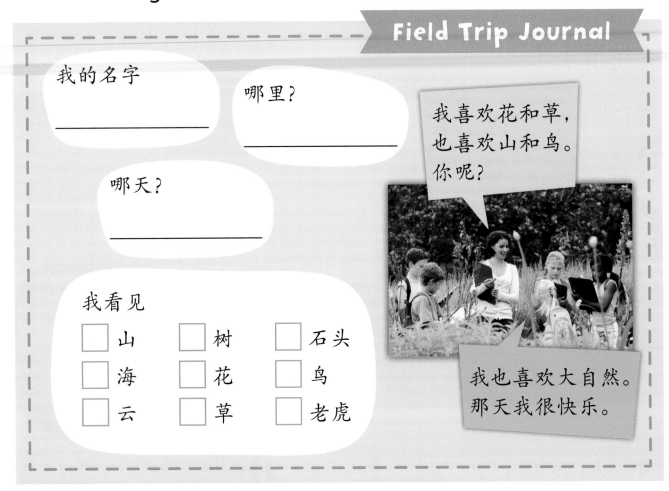

Field Trip Journal

我的名字

_____

哪里?

_____

哪天?

_____

我喜欢花和草，也喜欢山和鸟。你呢?

我也喜欢大自然。那天我很快乐。

我看见

☐ 山　　☐ 树　　☐ 石头

☐ 海　　☐ 花　　☐ 鸟

☐ 云　　☐ 草　　☐ 老虎

Game

Help the caterpillar get to the grass and talk to the frog. Circle 鱼 in the pond.

Song

🎧 **05** Listen and sing.

大自然真大。

天上有云，

云下有山，

山下有海，

海旁有地。

地上有石头，

有树、花和草，

还有小小的我们。

课堂用语 Classroom language

我可以去厕所吗？
May I go to the washroom, please?

用一用？

我可以用一用吗？
May I use it, please?

1 Review and trace the strokes.

丿 ㇆ 乚 乚

2 Learn the component. Trace ⺾ to complete the characters.

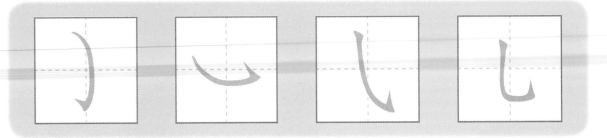

⺾ 花 苗 茶 菇

3 Colour ⺾ for fruits red, for vegetables green and for flowers orange.

香蕉　　菇　　葡萄

茄子　　苹果　　菊花　　茶花

4 Trace and write the characters.

一 十 艹 艹 艼 花 花

花 花

一 十 艹 艹 苎 苎 苗 苜 草

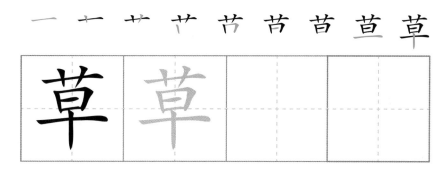

草 草

5 Write and say.

绿色的是树和 ☐ ，红

色、黄色、白色的是 ☐ 。

汉字小常识 Did you know?

Colour the characters in any colour you like.

In some characters, several components merge with one another to form a single structure.

 来 夹 爽 夷

多元学习 Connections

Cultures

China is a big country with spectacular landscapes. Look at the pictures and talk about these places with your friend.

Guangxi

这里的山和水真好看。

Shandong

我喜欢看云。

Yunnan

这些是山还是石头？

Inner Mongolia

天真蓝，草地真绿。

Zhejiang

花很好看。

Hong Kong

这里有山有海。

Project

1. Work with your friend. Match the pictures to the correct words. Then tell your friend which picture you like the most and why.

冷 _____

热 _____

高山 _____

大海 _____

大树 _____

草地 _____

2. Draw a scenic place and tell your friend why it is a good place to visit.

温习 Checkpoint

1 Help Hao Hao finish his travel scrapbook so he can tell his friends about his holiday.

我在天上。天真高，海真大。

十月，不冷也不热。

它在哪里？它在＿＿上。

蓝色的＿＿，白色的云，很好看。

我喜欢大自然，山上有树和＿＿，山下有海和小石头。

树上有小小的＿＿。

2 Work with your friend. Colour the stars and the chillies.

Words	说	读	写
天	☆	☆	🌶
地	☆	☆	🌶
云	☆	☆	🌶
山	☆	☆	☆
海	☆	☆	🌶
花	☆	☆	☆
草	☆	☆	☆
小	☆	☆	🌶
真	☆	☆	🌶
树	☆	🌶	🌶
石头	☆	🌶	🌶

Words and sentences	说	读	写
冷	☆	🌶	🌶
热	☆	🌶	🌶
大自然	☆	🌶	🌶
蓝色的天， 白色的云。	☆	🌶	🌶
天真高，海真大。	☆	🌶	🌶

Talk about mother nature	☆

3 What does your teacher say?

My teacher says ...

分享 Sharing

Words I remember

天	tiān	sky
地	dì	land
云	yún	cloud
山	shān	mountain
海	hǎi	sea
花	huā	flower
草	cǎo	grass
小	xiǎo	small
真	zhēn	really
树	shù	tree
石头	shí tou	rock

冷	lěng	cold
热	rè	hot
大自然	dà zì rán	nature

Other words

分开	fēn kāi	to separate
海水	hǎi shuǐ	sea water
地面	dì miàn	ground
还有	hái yǒu	also
奇妙	qí miào	wonderful

OXFORD
UNIVERSITY PRESS

Oxford University Press is a department of the University of Oxford.
It furthers the University's objective of excellence in research, scholarship,
and education by publishing worldwide. Oxford is a registered trade mark of
Oxford University Press in the UK and in certain other countries

Published in Hong Kong by
Oxford University Press (China) Limited
39th Floor, One Kowloon, 1 Wang Yuen Street, Kowloon Bay,
Hong Kong

Illustrated by Anne Lee, KK Ng, KY Chan and Wildman

Photographs for reproduction permitted by Dreamstime.com

China National Publications Import & Export (Group) Corporation is an authorized distributor of
Oxford Elementary Chinese.

Please contact content@cnpiec.com.cn or 86-10-65856782

ISBN: 978-0-19-082202-6

10 9 8 7 6 5 4 3 2